Wickhead's Guide to Verbal Gusto

Enriched and Enhanced Second Edition

Jim Kelly

Austin, Texas

Wickhead's Guide to Verbal Gusto
Enriched and Enhanced Second Edition
By Jim Kelly

© Jim Kelly, 2007, 2008, 2013. 2015
Wickhead's Guide to Verbal Gusto

Published by
Groundbreaking Press
8305 Arboles Circle
Austin, TX 78737
www.groundbreaking.com

Library of Congress Control Number: 2007930656
ISBN: 0-9793542-0-X

Second Edition

Senior Editor
Barbara Foley

Editor
Brad Fregger

Cover Production
M. Kevin Ford

Illustrator
Bob Cooksey

Original Wickhead Image
Chris Courson

Surf terms courtesy of Riptionary.com

All rights reserved. No part of this book may be reproduced or utilized in any form or by any means, electronic, or mechanical, including photocopying, or recording, or by an information storage and retrieval system, without permission in writing from the Author; unless, of course, you're dishing a compliment to a crewbie.

Something Great to Give

Give somebody a candid compliment and its influence can last for years, maybe a lifetime. But just because it comes from the heart doesn't preclude a little topspin. That's where this offbeat opus sallies forth. Why fore? Forsooth, it puts at your nimble fingertips synapse-stimulating words and concepts which aid your supple mind in tapping your soaring intellect to create the vibration refreshing ... my liege.

All this results not only in you generating compliments with artistic flair, but also in you being catapulted to the status of writer extraordinaire at your zenith. So, the next time you run across someone who deserves a genuine compliment, go ahead and step up to the plate for the creative side and crack one over the fence. It not only feels great, it deposits psychic income into your account with the universe.

Contributors and Influences

GOD	Monty Python	Eckhart Tolle
Alfred E. Newman	Dan Akroid	Laura Hildabran
Cervantes	Joe Carr	Julia Cameron
Groucho	Amy Goodman	Chez Jives
Scoop Nisker	Cheech the Peach	Corsalamule
Rosalie	Peter Sagal	Roger and Junko
Big Rick	Charlie Chan	The Larson Clan
Wheats	P. Yogananda	Eddie the Cat
Hacketto	Coach Jackson	Billy Connolly
D.S	Chuck	Prunellapea
Chan Werno	Larry Negevin	The Beta House
BG	St. Philip Neri	Barbara Foley
The Fish	Shelprock	Brad Fregger
C. Flag	Walt Whitman	Ann Herbert
Victor Hugo	John Wooden	Michael Dirda
The Connor Lads	Kip Addotta	Triple Threat Hake
James West	Janelle	The Bard of Avalon
Artemus Gordon	Brian Murphy	Cool Hand Luke
Woody Allen	Will Ferrel	Untold Others

Author's Preface

I believe it was Aristotle, or one of those other cagey veterans roving around Athens, who remarked, "Art should be both edifying and entertaining." One hastens to agree with this pith from the Parthenon, especially if applied to the "art of the compliment," that often overlooked and grossly underrated act of dishing a cohort a creative tribute.

Indeed, a cleverly crafted commendation boosts the vibes of everyone: you, me, Flipper, Sasquatch, the whole shebang. I contend this milieu could use more of 'em.

Ergo, I slapped together this praise-provoking portfolio to assist one in constructing creative kudos.

Specimens in point ...

> ... **He's a crack professional at the apex of his game.**
>
> ... **The commissioner of can do.**
>
> ... **Chevalier in the legion of skookum.**

It's semantic sunshine that'll help brighten any day, and this gem you hold in your hand makes it easy as "Ah-one-ah and ah-two-ah, thank you boys-za." That's because herein lies a passel of possible combinations, plus the old fill-in-the-blank trick, with (samples) in parentheses. All you do is mix, match, and fill in until it feels right, or you're struck by the giggleypoos.

So go ahead and loosen it up the next time you toast a family dignitary, pen a birthday salutation, or leave a voice mail. Simply ponder the person's positive traits, take a spin through these pages, then slip 'em the upper.

You'll surprise yourself on how inventive you are and how sweet it feels. Plus you'll know deep down, the first time you dish someone a verbal jewel, that it's a rare and mysterious form of beauty. May the *bon mot* be with you.

Perhaps a few tableaus will better illustrate the point.

For instance:

You could tell your girlfriend she looks great. Or, you could sprinkle in a dash of verbal spice, and say ...

You're resplendent beyond regulations and as radiant as a Nassau Sunrise. Plus, I might add, the creme de la creme, no whip!

Note:

Why just say it when you can paint a picture?

Or, perhaps:

You're at the computer and a pesky ad keeps popping up. You could ask your computer-whiz son for help for the umpteenth time, or, you could stay loose, write tight,

and inquire ...

My good and skillful offspring, since you are renowned and revered throughout the hood as the Commodore of Communication, might you be able to jettison this ad into the ocean blue?

Note:

Combine thoughts from any page to fit the situation. There's no order. It's your order. That's half the fun.

And, wouldn't you know …

You've just noticed there's no hot water in the house; time to call your handyman husband. But alas, you get his voicemail.

The perfect time for …

Hark, noble husband, tis I, yon wife, and forsooth, the royal water heater appears to no longer be "all systems go." Perhaps, when the affairs of state permit, you could inspect the once bubbling cauldron and insight its triumphant return of warmth to the castle's frosty faucets.

I bid you a sans BTU adieu.

Note:

When you run across words in parentheses, remember they're just suggestions. You can use 'em or fill in your own for a creative hootenanny that's more inspiring than Maverick doing a 4G inverted dive with a Mig 28.

Wickhead
June, 2015

Table of Contents

Contributors and Influences _____ V

Author's Preface _____ VII

Table of Contents _____ XV

Ladies _____ 1

Gentlemen _____ 33

High-Spirited Youth _____ 63

Syllables from Surfology _____ 79

Positive Vibes for Whom Have You _____ 85

Glossary _____ 109

Author's Bio _____ 155

"If you want to lift yourself up, lift up someone else."

— Booker T. Washington

Ladies

Ladies

Lady of (the Manor).

Maiden with (moxie).

Looks like a million (up-front, cash).

Noted (educator).

Champion of the (oppressed).

Magnet for (good).

Wickhead's Guide to Verbal Gusto

Buoyant and captivating.

(Fraulein) executing the
(waterskiing at dawn) dynamic.

Catch her dazzling highlights on
(The Ocho).

Tanned, buffed, and (chuffed).

Walking (rainbow) with a
sun-kissed body.

Hoisting sail on
(a new adventure).

Dr. (Mom).

Imbued with (motherly) wisdom.

A trusted guide through life's
(moral thickets and ethical swamps).

Paragon of (professionalism).

Thinking audaciously and
acting (courageously).

Ms. (Make It Happen).

Wickhead's Guide to Verbal Gusto

Vital and (vigorous).

Lady who plans the work then (works the plan).

Taking a bullet train to (Success City) and getting off at (Easy street).

(Blast) of fresh air.

Lass without a mean bone in her (magnificent) body.

Yet again (perpetrating random kindness and committing senseless acts of beauty).

Ladies

Beloved (spouse).

(Baroness) Bravisimo and (beauty) bellissimo.

One of the most celebrated (domestic goddesses) of our time.

Born (entrepreneur).

Cloudburst of (creativity).

Marketing (soothsayer) who has (daily epiphanies).

Oasis of (fresh ideas).

Designing products both
(fanciful and functional).

Her address is:
(Suite One, The Leading Edge).

One of the best and the brightest.

Light on her feet, quick with
her wits.

Poet laureate of (Gotham).

Ladies

Trail blazing (visionary).

Revolutionizing the world and changing the course of (history).

Has the right stuff (and some left over).

Svelte and (shapely).

Sparkling beacon of (off-the-beaten-path) elegance.

A franchise player in the game of (fashion).

Second to none.

Friend and (inspiration).

Woman who knows a solid bet is
(to bet on herself).

The Princess of (Pilates).

Tres chic (mademoiselle).

Ravishing as a
(San Francisco) sunset.

Ladies

Eurhythmic First Lady of
(modern dance).

Winner for (artistic) achievement.

Headed to Xanadu to
(shake her tambourine).

(Grandma) with gumption.

Pulling (empowerment) out
of her bag of tricks.

Lives by the motto:
(goodness is the only investment that
never fails).

Proactive woman of (action).

(Interior designing) tour de force.

Coined the decluttering declaration: (feng-schwait-a-minute).

Charming and (vivacious).

Spontaneous, soulful and (sagacious).

Lady who brings it!

Ladies

Lass making her own (luck).

Using the (Law of Attraction) to take
the dip out of serendipity.

Her (very presence) is auspicious.

It's (Tony) No Baloney, a.k.a.
(the persona sans bologna).

(Lass) of (talents) untold.

Devisor of the (solution sweet)
with the (prudent proviso).

Medicine (woman) of the earth.

(Physician) extraordinaire.

(Jam out) on the power and intelligence of herbs.

Dexterous (chiropractor) with the touch of (a Swiss watchmaker).

Promulgator of (propitious postures).

Lady who will sync your (chakras).

Ladies

Spontaneous and (adventurous).

Go to (gal).

Certified (answer woman) embracing (tempest fugit so carpe diem).

(Female) with focus.

Fountain of knowledge.

Guided by her (moral) compass, (spiritual) gyroscope and (creative) glockenspiel.

Wickhead's Guide to Verbal Gusto

Dame Commander of the (kitchen).

International leader in the development of (scrump meals).

Concocting a (movable) feast replete with majesty, pageantry and, of course, (Waldorf salad).

Smooth, suave, and (sophisticated).

Cool, calm, and (collected).

(Supervisor) capable of (Delphic utterances).

Ladies

Lovely and (talented).

(Roommate) swift of mind and foot.

Back from a (triumphant) mission where she reached the zenith of (fab-boo).

(Travel Agent) in the first echelon.

Stretching the mind with (stimulating) ideas.

She includes the (Bluebird of Happiness) at no additional charge.

Citizen of (the universe).

Architect of (her own destiny).

Fears not change because without it (there would be no butterflies).

Lady possessing (uncommon assets).

Unleashing the forces of (creativity, imagination, and enterprise).

Doesn't just car pool—she conducts a mobile (happiness) summit.

Ladies

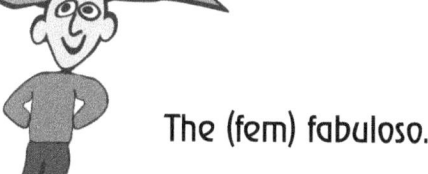

The (fem) fabuloso.

Queen of (kindheartedness).

Beloved (benefactor to the bambinos).

My (bedazzling) most excellent (wife).

The fairest flower of femininity.

Knows two clutch requirements of a happy life are: (1. An attitude of gratitude, and 2. Gotta have more cowbell baby!).

(Resplendent) beyond regulations.

Lovely as a (lotus blossom).

Lass who looks mar-vel-ous to the
(5th power and 6th sense).

Teacher (deluxe).

Turns (setbacks) to her
add-von-tage.

Agrees with Helen Keller:
(Life is a daring adventure, or nothing).

Windswept (woman).

Shimmering
(wakeboarding) ar-teest.

Rewriting the owner's manual
on (aquatic) chic.

Illustrious and (industrious).

Lady (unlimited).

Countervails (complacency)
with charm, style, and (veteran moves).

(Babysitter) and Charge'd'affairs
vested with plenipotentiary powers.

Uniquely qualified
(in a number of dimensions).

Parlaying leftovers into (fusion tacos)
fit for the Earl of (Chowhound).

From Siberia to the (Serengeti), from Tasmania to
(Terra del Fuego).

She's the hostess with the mostess dishing out a
(smorgasbord of sweetness).

Woman whose (vibrations) go beyond (good)
into the mystical.

Olympic caliber (soccer mom).

Chef (cordon blue).

Her universally celebrated (sandwiches) are the (coup de chow).

Matriculating (Matriarch).

Following (Her) bliss and closing the gap.

Preferred and (aperitif), bold and expressive, yet unassuming and approachable.

Strikingly (attractive).

(Walks) in a rarified realm.

Lady laden with (shibumi).

Toast of the (town).

Woman of the (hour).

Here's looking at you, kid.

Ladies

Melodious (diva).

(Vocalist) in the vanguard of the vanguard.

Rocking beyond (reproach).

Superchick.

Knows problems are opportunities
in work clothes.

Consistently boots out doubt thereby
(expanding her vistas to embrace
endless possibilities).

Wickhead's Guide to Verbal Gusto

Local (heroine).

Student athlete and (academic all-star).

Credit to the solar system (as Kepler and Galileo knew it, along with recent telemetry from the Jet Propulsion Laboratory).

Kindred spirit.

Off to a (galloping) start.

Fomenting a (prosperity) counterrevolution.

Ladies

Eminent country (playwrite).

(Balmy zephyr) in
a heat wave.

Her (decisions) are
saturated with heads-up-ness.

Performance proven.

Canny (consumer).

Nipping (buyer's remorse) in the bud
with (carpe refundum).

Woman of (warmth).

Gravitates towards (goodness).

Lives with a song in her heart, smile on her face, and the intuitive knowledge of just when to (rend the air with song).

(Girl) with game.

(Gal) with (her) groove on.

On a (soul) safari.

Ladies

The one and only.

My elegant and classy (daughter).

Casting cares to the wind
('cause it's a summertime thang).

Refreshingly (unorthodox).

Lass who (cliff-dived with Elvis
in Acapulco) then blew kisses
to the crowd.

The Countess of (Chutzpah).

Enchanting (prima ballerina).

A ballet step beyond (brilliant).

She's the (creme de la creme) no whip.

Woman of (vision).

Lady of (letters).

Advisor to (presidents).

Invaluable (confidante).

A purveyor of
(spiritual refreshment).

A lady who rates high on any scale.

(Indomitable) optimist.

Handles life's (curve balls)
with elan, aplomb, and savior faire.

Turns (lemons) into (lemonade),
serves it in a (frosted mug),
then whimsically frolicks.

"Kind words can be short and easy to speak, but their echoes are truly endless."
- Mother Teresa

Gentlemen

Wickhead's Guide to Verbal Gusto

Gentlemen

Chief of (Naval) Operations.

Charting a course for action, adventure, and (romance).

One hell of a model (American).

My distinguished (brother).

At the apogee of his (plumbing) skill set.

Displaying the courage and cachet of (Don Quixote De La Mancha).

Chef (Dad).
on the dawn patrol.

Slinging (hash) beyond compare.

Replicating a (restaurant) experience
at a fraction of the price.

The Commissioner of (can-do).

Dean of
(doing the impossible).

Composing another (aesthetic triumph).

Gentlemen

The pro from (Sheboygan).

Czar of par.

His (swing) has the fluid grace of (a condor in flight).

The Mahatma of (motivation).

Captain of (industry).

Drops a negative vibe like (a two-foot putt).

Daring and (dashing).

Fearless (leader).

Rescuer of (damsels) in distress.

_____

Man of (steel).

Samurai of (fitness).

Possesses the strength of (1000 woolly mammoths).

Gentlemen

The Archduke of (action).

Co-chair of the (go for it) caucus.

Concurs with Henry Ford that (obstacles are those dreadful things you see when you take your eyes off your goal).

(Computer) wizard from parts unknown.

Getting jiggy with (the new system).

Transformed his keyboard into (a swift cat boat on the digital ocean).

Back by (popular) demand.

Direct from a (bodacious) world tour.

The (guy) whose (insight)
gives me a bigger smile than
(a possum with a sweet potato).

Multifaceted, multilingual, and
multi-(competent).

Multi (man).

(Folk) hero
whose (boot heels) are wanderin'.

Gentlemen

(Boyfriend) who holds a black belt in (boo-ya!).

Chortles at (challenges), chuckles at (fear).

Living an (action adventure).

Definitive (wet boater) and mythical (sea dog).

Raising the sails to catch the (nimble) gales.

Lives by the nautical wisdom (balance is the key and water is your friend).

Enlightened (cogitator).

Staying forever (young).

Celebrating the 30th anniversary of his (20th birthday).

Admiral of (adventure).

Earl of (excitement).

Field commander of (farfugnuggen).

(Irishman) at large.

Epicenter of seismic (positive vibes).

In the right place, at the right time, with the (heezy fo' sheezy).

International ambassador of (good will).

Member of the (intelligentsia).

Agrees with philosophers a true wise man knows nothing, however, when meditating, (a whole lotta nothin' can be a real cool hand).

(Husband) who rides tall in the saddle and casts a shadow of (integrity).

Soaring with (eagles).

Yet again choosing (good over greed).

Indefatigable and (awe-inspiring).

Supreme Allied Commander of (cleaning the garage).

Keeping it swank, not dank.

Gentlemen

Mr. (No Negs).

Promulgating paradigm shifting (positives).

Galvanizing (inspired action).

Rough, tough, and hard to bluff.

Displaying (panache) under pressure.

Drives an (Austin Martin DB-5 with modifications), the (ejector seat) alone has gotten' him out of (many-a-jam).

The right honorable ...

(Douglas) T. Firefly (Stevenson).

(History) buff who applauds (the Trojan horse as one of the best ruses of the bronze age).

Philanthropic and (altruistic).

Gallant (knight errant).

Roaming the (countryside) seeking (adventures) to prove his chivalry.

Gentlemen

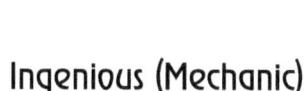

Ingenious (Mechanic).

On the threshold of a
(technological) breakthrough.

The only man known who can
(start) the Golden (lawn mower)
of Mambreeno.
[with apologies to Cervantes]

Intrepid and (steadfast).

(Alternative energy)
activist with street cred.

Miner of
(thin air diamonds).

High rolling (wheeler-dealer).

A primal force of (nature).

Embarking on another sojourn to (success).

Napoleonic figure marshaling a creative assault on the (bastions of boredom).

Riveting (conversationalist) whose speeches to his kids rank high in the annals of (oratory).

Following his uncanny instinct to (a garage sale where he uncovered the original deed to the Louisiana Purchase).

Gentlemen

Sage from the (South).

As tough and romantic
as the city he loves.

Exercising the franchise on
election day.

(Personal trainer)
firing on all cylinders.

Converts a marathon into
(one mile 26 times).

The man who can and did and
(will do it again).

Wickhead's Guide to Verbal Gusto

Consummate (cosmopolitan) in a (teaming metropolis).

Viceroy of (vim, vigor, and vitamins).

Senses something (boom brottus) this way comes.

———————————————

Kosher, Hamish (Mensch).

Voted most likely to (be told mazeltov).

Agrees with Groucho, time flies like an arrow, fruit flies like a banana.

Gentlemen

Swashbuckling and (flamboyant).

(Marketing) maven.

Dreams no Lilliputian (dreams).

Stepping
(unto the breach once again).

(Lucky) because he's (plucky).

That rare breed that can go against all
odds without getting (flummoxed).

(Blues) icon.

Riffin' cool grooves
and stretched out jams.

Appreciates a coolwater sandwich
and a Sunday go to meetin' bun.

Bohemian (intellectual).

Once again unmuzzling (ripe) wisdom.

When asked directions has been known to cite
(the ancient Greek geographer Strabo).

Gentlemen

Wing commander (Driftwood).

Steaming through (obstacles) at flank speed.

Has in his possession the (magic wandoo).

Tribune of (client service).

Doesn't work harder, works smarter.

The best of the best (if not more so).

Prestigious and (influential).

Erudite (constitutional) scholar.

Possesses a treasure trove of (pertinent knowledge).

___

Down hard and (hard down).

Juggernaut of (soul).

Knows if at first you don't succeed, hire (Chuck Norris).

Gentlemen

(Web) Houdini.

Commodore of communication.

Seer of the (future).

My learned (colleague).

Myriad minded (author, historian)
and horse for the course.

His ideas are upper-deck home runs.

Wickhead's Guide to Verbal Gusto

(His) Excellency.

Award-winning (humorist) and astute (political analyst).

One of the most esteemed (neighbors) known to mankind.

Blithe-spirited.

Duke of (doing it right).

Knows you can't keep a (good man) down.

Gentlemen

All around (nice guy).

Working for a great metropolitan (newspaper).

(Grabbing for gusto) in a gusto world.

Seasoned (gourmand).

A savant at concocting a (savory flavor profile).

One of the best minds in the country at (ordering dinner).

Wickhead's Guide to Verbal Gusto

Romantic (bard).

(Troubadour) in residence.

Projecting (saulubrious) vibrations.

Stouthearted warrior-chieftain.

A (creative) operator.

Known to underwrite an (expedition) not only with shekels and drachmas but also (gold sovereigns recovered in shallow water off Key West).

Gentlemen

Omnipotent (technician).

Raja of (remodeling).

Has the tools, has (the talent).

(Rural) legend.

In peek (physical) condition.

Can whip his weight (in wildcats).

Paladin of (pumping iron).

Quintessential (jock of all sport).

Runs like (the wind).

_____

Triple threat (Hake).

Game-shifting (receiver).

Has the situational awareness of (an air traffic controller in spikes).

(Creative) hombre.

Bidding farewell to
(pesky limiting beliefs).

Possesses the transcendent
insight of the (unshackled).

(Man) who bestrides life like
a colossus.

Keeps (his) game tight.

Concurs with (Socrates) that
(we must escape from the cave of
illusions) post haste, if not sooner.

Wickhead's Guide to Verbal Gusto

"I can live for two months on a good compliment."
— Mark Twain

High-Spirited Youth

High-Spirited Youth

Square shooting.

Consensus All-American (teenager).

Taking the A train to (the honor role).

The (dude) dynamic.

(His) exploits are known throughout the (universe).

(He) changed the game of Horse, with the upper atmosphere, over the roof shot.

Wickhead's Guide to Verbal Gusto

Young and aspiring.

(Bake sale) tycoons.

Keeping a hawk eye on
supply and demand, not to mention
(the strength of the Euro).

(Galaxy) class.

All systems go.

Cosmic voyager with all
(his) wookies in a row.

Little (slugger).

Choosing heads-up (fruits and veggies) at the training table.

(He) knows eating smart makes (him) strong like bull!

(Richly) talented.

Vaunted (instrumentalist).

Considered among the world's golden-toned (kazoo players).

Wickhead's Guide to Verbal Gusto

(Fad) generating.

Princess of (Pizzazz).

A (senorita) that has at her command (dose languages).

Impeccably (dressed).

Having an epic (hair) day.

Crown prince of the (casual North Pole look).

Rising Star.

Prestigious (prestidigitator).

The amazing (wunderkind).

(Boy) scout whose uniform is plastered with merit badges.

Living scout values of being (trustworthy, loyal, helpful, friendly, courteous, kind, obedient, cheerful, thrifty, brave, clean, humble, and reverent).

A scout without (doubt).

The little (Duchess) of (data).

Hitting (her) stride.

Maintaining (normal) cool
in the face of the
(glitch) of the century.

Jaunty (fashion) pioneer.

On the cutting edge of
(teen couture).

Featuring a (hat) that's unsurpassed.

Peerless and (at the ready).

(Prodigy) on the premises.

One of the most
(heads-up) kids in the (vicinity).

Voon-der-bar.

Jet propelled (juvenile).

Bringing (dreams) to life.

Little (giant).

Performing feats beyond the imagination.

Leaving (ordinary) behind and living for (greatness).

Rad (lad).

Trickin' (moves).

Grindin' (rails).

High-Spirited Youth

(Teen) phenom.

(Microchip) magician.

Greased lightning
(on any keyboard).

Turbocharged, (skateboarding) enthusiast.

Turning in another (bravura) performance.

When the heat's on (he's) cooler than
(a cucumber patch in Siberia).

(8th) grade dynamo.

Lusting for life.

Creating (dance moves) that'll someday be in the Smithsonian.

Enterprising (little chap).

Hard-driving (dude sickle).

Who came, who saw, who (mowed), and (got paid handsomely).

High-Spirited Youth

Incipient (bon vivant).

Budding (epicure).

Orders (his) chocolate milk shaken, not stirred.

Adroit (youngster).

(Working) with ardor and (alacrity).

(Delivering papers) with the speed of (Pegasus).

Wickhead's Guide to Verbal Gusto

Bee's knees and (cat's pajamas).

Cuter than (a speckled puppy sleeping under a red wagon).

Ultra-talented brain child.

High Panjandrum of (setting trends).

(Several weeks) ahead of (his) time.

Popular (guy) drinking a popular beverage at a popular price.

High-Spirited Youth

Inimitable but never (diminutive).

(Backpacking) scholar.

Using (her) library card to
(unlock the mysteries of the universe).

———————————————

Young buckaroo of
(sweeping enthusiasms).

Chip off the old block.

Paraphrasing (Goethe) with:
Great (tree house) architecture
is frozen music, albeit swaying slightly.

Wickhead's Guide to Verbal Gusto

"Be excellent to one another."
- Bill and Ted

Syllables from Surfology

Syllables from Surfology

(Living) legend.

Jazzing the glass.

Chairing a one (man) board meeting in the (green room).

(Woman) of the waves.

The Diva of (double-overhead).

(Babe) in the barrel.

Soul (surfer).

Flying down the line
with the (X factor).

Time traveling through a
(tapioca twizzler).

Radolescent.

(Ripping) rail to rail.

Shooting the (smurf barrel)
in Conan style.

Swami of the (swells).

(Waterman) in a squid lid
taking off on the (tastiest) of tubes.

Getting (bowled, shacked, and barreled)
in the alchemy hour.

(Wahini) of many wonders.

Chilaxing with (her) crewbies.

Hearing (tubular bells) in the
(Church of the Open Sky).

"Marge, you're as pretty as Princess Leia and as smart as Yoda."

- Homer Simpson

Positive Vibes for Whom Have You

Positive Vibes for Whom Have You

Leading authority on
(fixing the problem).

Renowned and revered
throughout (this great land).

Knows the most succinct
cosmic phrase ever uttered is
… What me worry?

Dauntless (sherpa).

(Snowboarding) virtuoso.

Heralded by
(500 gleaming trumpets).

Wickhead's Guide to Verbal Gusto

Noble minded and (lion hearted).

Unsung (humanitarian).

Paying it forward.

Renaissance (coach).

Lives by the creed:
(A positive attitude pays you,
a negative one costs you).

Teaches: (Things turn out best for the people who make the best of how things turn out).

Considerate and (conscientious).

Child of God.

Knows where the treasure's buried.

(Employer) of unusual merit.

M. V. P. at (catching people doing things right).

Setting the gold standard for a (cool place to work).

Inwardly (guided).

Steward of the (land).

Skillful (collaborator with nature).

One of life's heroes.

In a league of (her) own.

Arch exponent of (aroma) therapy.

Wiley (veteran).

Heeds the council of (the Gusto Report).

Can't get enough of (trampoline badminton) on The Ocho.

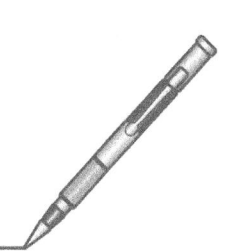

The one and only.

Sultan of (solutions).

Initiating a legendary (gusto) moment.

My perspicacious (protégé).

(Mastermind) for the job.

(His) work reflects the nimble touch of the (maestro).

(Critically) acclaimed.

New (man) in the pantheon displaying an impressive (cannon of work).

Holds a post doctoral degree in (Yankee know-how).

Buffed, ripped, and (chiseled).

Accredited (Hercules).

Just clocked a
(10,000 jigawatt workout).

(Karaoke) mogul.

Pulling the chalks on
(a flight of fancy).

One (lady) brain trust.

Maxin' and relaxin'.

(Chauffeur) and ship's chandler.

Currently on sabbatical to study
that classic maneuver
(The Klink dipsy-doodle).

The (man) with
(the deal that appeals).

Founding another dynamic (enterprise).

Using the tried and true formula of
(high hopes and low overhead).

Undisputed and (top-ranked).

Going for gold.

(Lass) who realizes adversity
is a stepping stone to
the plateau of greatness.

Top (banana) at the peak of
(ripeness).

(Man) who ordered
an embargo on (boredom).

Knows at the philosopher's café
you get the (Blue Plato Special).

Wickhead's Guide to Verbal Gusto

Parents with (poise).

Giving their kids roots,
wings, and (tower clearance).

Rockin' in the U.S.A.

Exalted (wife).

At the summit of her (cooking game).

Garnering rave reviews for (her)
signature dish (Noodles Boom Brottus).

The (cook) with the look that cooks.

The instantaneous (gourmet).

Concoctor of delicacies (propitious, nutritious, and delicious).

(Class act) for the ages.

Making (optimism) a way of life.

Knows (laughter) is the sun that drives winter from the human face.

Cagey (cohort).

Comrade in (comedy).

The master of (mirth).

The Prime Minister of (PMA).

Founding father of (reverse skepticism).

Specialist at shifting (bummers) into retrograde.

Offbeat (health) guru.

Busting a move on (blueberries).

Knows you need the right (pit) strategy to get to the victory lane in the human race.

Gallant and (heroic).

(Undersea) explorer.

Sallying forth (whilst submerged).

Patron of the (sporting green).

Valedictorian of the (bleachers).

Illuminating guide to existential (parking at Wrigley).

Restless (sculptor).

Applying the (coup de grace).

Revealing (the piece de resistance).

Dashing and (debonair).

Argonaut with (dexterous) hands and a (supple) mind.

Tastefully continuing through the space-time continuum.

Indubitably bodacious (showman).

Hurtling toward incalculable (distinction).

Would give (P.T. Barnum) a run for the roses.

Wickhead's Guide to Verbal Gusto

My pithy (piasano) the (chow) pundit.

Current director of (lunch) research.

Successfully led the (Chicago) mission to (Billy Goat—where you can butt in anytime).

Young at heart.

The (editor) refreshing.

Knows there's no touch like (a finishing) touch.

Hale and hearty.

World class (skier).

Stimulating (her) (cerebellum) by carving (double black diamonds).

Agile (strategist).

(Man) of mark.

Currently rendezvousing with (relaxation).

The (Honolulu) humdinger.

Catalyst in shifting
(planetary) awareness.

Knows every thought creates,
(so make those synapses sweet).

Globe (trotting).

(Man) for all seasons.

Just posted-up with (the mojo).

Mr. and Mrs. (On-the-Ball).

They possess a preternatural ability to be (way cool).

A couple that knows today is a gift that's why it's called the present.

Crackerjack (salesgirl) doing exceptional work.

Exceeding all (expectations).

(Her) career trajectory is headed (to the heliopause).

Lady whose (large as life
and twice as sassy).

(Her) X-Ray vision can see
quantums of good in a bad situation.

(Her) positive attitude magically
changes (a narley uh-oh) into
easy breezy.

Beautiful, urbane and (charismatic).

Futurist and (bibliophile).

Holding forth on
(string theory in 10-dimensional hyper space).

Immeasurable life force.

Saturated with infinite creative potential.

At <u>this</u> very moment.

Unlimited spiritual being having a human experience.

Extension of Source Energy.

Knows despite current appearances, we're all in the same love bath!

"Feeling gratitude and not expressing it is like wrapping a present and not giving it."

- William Arthur Ward

Forsooth the Glossary

"If you're in a pinch to hustle a birthday card into an envelope, just flip through the glossary. The right words will rush to your side my liege."

Notage

Glossary

ACUMEN – Accuracy and keenness of judgment or insight.

ACCOLADE – An expression of approval; praise. A special acknowledgement; an award.

ACCREDITED – Has credentials or authority; authorized.

ACQUIRED – To gain possession of: "to fortunately acquire 10 copies of Wickhead."

ACTUALIZE – To realize in action or make real; to become actual.

ADEPT – Very skilled; proficient, an expert.

ADIEU – Good by; farewell.

ADROIT – Dexterous; deft. Skillful and adept under pressing conditions.

AD-VON-TAGE – Advantage.

AERIAL – (surfing) The part of a maneuver where a surfer and his board leave the water.

AESTHETIC – Of or concerning the appreciation of beauty or good taste.

AFICIONADO – An enthusiastic admirer or follower; a devotee.

AGILE – Characterized by quickness, lightness, and ease of movement. Nimble; mentally alert; "an agile mind."

AHOY – A general greeting. A call used in hailing a person or vessel.

AIDE DE CAMP – A military officer acting as secretary and confidential assistant to a superior officer of general or flag rank. An aide.

ALACRITY – Cheerful willingness, speed, or quickness.

ALCHEMY HOUR – (surfing) The period of time when a surfer enjoys the best a wave has to offer. The result is a magical feeling that touches the soul and gives the surfer a bigger smile than a possum with a sweet potato.

ALTRUISTIC – Unselfish concern for the welfare of others; selflessness.

AMIGO – (Spanish) Friend.

AMPED – Fired up, stoked, psyched.

APEX – The highest point: "the apex of a hill."

APLOMB – Self-confident assurance; poise.

APPRISED – To be informed.

ARCHITECT – One who designs, plans, or devises.

Glossary

ARCH EXPONENT – The chief person who speaks for, represents, or advocates a position.

ARDOR – Fiery intensity of feeling; passion.

ARGONAUT – A person who is engaged in a dangerous but rewarding quest; an adventurer.

ARISTOTLE – Greek philosopher, pupil of Plato, and tutor of Alexander the Great.

ARRAY – An orderly arrangement.

AU CURRANT – (Spanish) Up on current affairs; informed of recent developments.

AUGUST – Inspiring awe or admiration; majestic: "The august presence of the monarch."

AUDACIOUS – Fearlessly daring, bold.

AUSPICIOUS – Attended by favorable circumstances; propitious: "an auspicious day for a picnic."

AVANT GARDE – (French) A group or person active in the invention and application of new techniques in a given field, esp. the arts..

AY CARAMBA – (Spanish) Darn! Heck!

BADMINTON – A sport played by volleying a shuttlecock back and forth over a high net by means of light, long-handled racket.

BALMY – Having the quality or fragrance of balm; soothing. Mild and pleasant: "a balmy breeze."

BALMY ZEPHER – A cool, pleasant breeze.

BAMBINO – A child, a baby.

BARD – A poet; especially a lyric poet.

BARON – A nobleman of continental Europe.

BARRISTER – A lawyer.

BEE'S KNEES – See cat's pajamas.

BELLA – (Italian) Good.

BELLISSMO – (Italian) Beautiful.

BENEFACTOR – One that gives aid, especially financial aid.

BESTRIDE – To sit or stand on with legs astride; straddle. To dominate by position; tower over.

BIBLIOPHILE – A lover of books. A collector of books.

BLING – showy jewelry.

BLISS – Extreme happiness; ecstasy. An inner vibe of joyful guidance.

BODACIOUS – Remarkable; prodigious; audacious; bold; gutsy.

Glossary

BOFFO – Extremely successful; great.

BOHEMIAN – A person with artistic or literary interests who disregards conventional standards.

BONA FIDE – Authentic; genuine; made or carried out in good faith; sincere.

BON MOT – A clever saying; a witticism.

BON VIVANT – A person with refined tastes that enjoys superb food and drink.

BOOM BROTTUS – Most excellent, if not more so.

BOO-YA – (Slang) Used to express enthusiasm, exuberance, or anything else for that matter.

BOWLED – See green room.

BRAND X – (Surfing) Anything of inferior quality.

BROLADEX – (Surfing) Where a guy keeps all his "bros" phone numbers; a cell phone.

BROSEF – (Surfing) A best friend.

BRAH – (Surfing) Surf brother, associate, peer, colleague, friend in liquid solidarity. In fact, anyone on the planet, including women.

BRAIN TRUST – A group of experts who serve, usually unofficially, as advisors and policy planners, especially in a government.

BRAVURA – Brilliant technique or style in performance.

BUDDHA – (Hawaiian Pidgin) Brother.

BUFFED – Being in fantastic physical shape with a body that looks marvelous.

BUENO – (Spanish) Good.

BURLEY DELIVERIES – A delivery that requires a strong, muscular person.

BURNT REYNOLDS – (Surfing) A guy who is badly sunburned.

BUSTING A MOVE – (Slang) Making a move.

BUST A MOVE – (Slang) Make a move.

BUYER'S REMORSE – Anguish arising after purchasing a product or service.

CACHET – A mark or quality of distinction, individuality, or authenticity.

CAGEY – Careful, crafty, shrewd.

CANDID – Sincere, honest.

Glossary

CANINE – Dog.

CANNY – Cautious and shrewd.

CAPTIVATING – To attract or hold by charm, beauty, or excellence.

CARBON FOOTPRINT – The amount of carbon dioxide an individual or organization produces.

CARPE DIEM – (Latin) Seize the day.

CAUCUS – A meeting of the local members of a political party.

CAT'S PAJAMAS – (Slang) Really good; the best.

CEREBELLUM – The part of the brain responsible for, among other things, posture and balance.

CHAKRAS – The seven centers of spiritual energy in the human body according to yoga philosophy.

CHARGE D'AFFAIRS – A diplomat or person who temporarily substitutes for an absent ambassador or minister.

CHARISMATIC – Possessing personal magnetism; charm.

CHAKRKAS – One of the seven centers of spiritual energy in the human body according to Yoga philosophy.

Wickhead's Guide to Verbal Gusto

CHARLIE CHAN – Inscrutable but unbeatable detective in a string of 50s flicks. He was known for peering into the heart of the problem and distilling it into a bon mot.

CHAUFFER – One employed to drive a private automobile or other means of conveyance such as a bicycle rickshaw, which might be found, for example, at a leading college like the University of Florida.

CHEF CORDON BLEU – A distinguished master chef.

CHEVALIER – A member of certain male orders of knighthood or merit, such as the Legion of Honor of France.

CHIC – Stylish and fashionable.

CHILLAX – To chill and relax simultaneously.

CHIMICHANGA – A deep-fried burrito.

CHIVALRY – The qualities idealized by knighthood, such as bravery, courtesy, honor, and gallantry toward woman.

CHOCK – A block or wedge placed under something to keep it from moving. Take for example, the wheels of an airplane.

CHORTLE – A snorting, joyful laugh or chuckle.

CHUFF – Whatever you want it to mean as long as it's positive. Some British band guy coined it.

Glossary

CHURCH OF THE OPEN SKY – The ocean and what one experiences when enjoying her magnificent aspects, be it surfing or other water-related activities.

CHUTZPAH – (Yiddish) Nerve; audacity.

CLUTCH – A tense, critical situation.

COGENT – Appealing to the intellect or powers of reasoning; convincing.

COGITATING – Thinking.

COHORT – A companion or associate.

COIN OF THE REALM – Currency or anything else that's valuable in a given location or environment.

COLLABORATE – To work together, especially in a joint intellectual effort.

COLOSSAL – Huge, immense, gargantuan.

COLOSSUS – A huge statue. Something likened to a huge statue in size or importance.

COLLEAGUE – A fellow member of a profession; an associate.

COMMODORE – The senior captain of a naval squadron.

COMPADRE – (Spanish) A friend.

Wickhead's Guide to Verbal Gusto

COMPLACENCY – Contented to a fault; self-satisfied and unconcerned.

COMRADE – A person who shares one's interests or activities; a friend or companion.

CONAN STYLE – (surfing) To attempt the impossible with the bravery of Conan the Barbarian.

CONCUR – To be of the same opinion; agree.

CONFIDANT – One to whom secrets and private matters are disclosed. A trusted friend.

CONNOISSEUR – A person with expert knowledge or training, especially in the fine arts. Someone with informed and discriminating tastes.

CONSCIENTIOUS – Guided by or in accordance with the dictates of conscience; principled.

CONSENSUS ALL-AMERICAN – Chosen by majority as the best amateur in the United States at a particular position.

CONSORT – A partner; companion. A spouse especially of a reigning king or queen..

CONSUMMATE – Supremely accomplished or skilled.

CONTEND – To maintain or assert.

CONTESSA – (Italian) A countess.

Glossary

CONVENTION – General agreement or acceptance of certain practices or attitudes.

COOLEO – Someone or something that is totally cool.

COOLWATER SANDWICH – (slang) a slice of watermelon.

CORDIALLY – Warmly and sincerely; friendly.

COSMOPOLITAN – So sophisticated as to be at home in all parts of the world or conversant with many spheres of interest – "a cosmopolitan traveler."

COUNTERVAIL – To act against with equal force; counteract.

COUP DE CHOW – Food that is, upon first bite, decisively Boom Brottus'.

COUTURE – The business of designing, making, and selling custom-made fashion for women. The high-fashion clothing created by designers.

COUPE DE GRACE – A finishing stroke or decisive event.

CRACKERJACK – Possessing first-rate ability.

CREME DE LA CREME – Something superlative. People of the highest social level.

CREWBIES – (Surfing) Close-knit group that surfs together, usually at the same spot, break, or area. The crew one hangs with.

Wickhead's Guide to Verbal Gusto

CREWMASTER – (Surfing) The one in a crew that always seems to be the organizer for a go-out, has the latest on what break is working, and generally rips when he's/she's on it.

CZAR – A male monarch or emperor. A person having great power.

DAPPER – Neat and stylish in dress.

DAME COMMANDER – A female commander.

DAMSEL – A young woman or girl; a maiden.

DANK – (Street slang) Extremely non-excellent.

DASHING – Gallant or spirited in attitude or dress.

DAUNTLESS – Incapable of being intimidated or discouraged; fearless.

DEBONAIR – Suave, urbane.

DEBUTANT – A young woman making a formal debut into society.

DEFINITIVE – Supplying or being a final statement or decision; conclusive.

DELPHIC – (Greek Mythology) Of or relating to Delphi or to the oracle of Apollo at Delphi.

DEPORTMENT – A manor of personal conduct; behavior.

Glossary

DE-VO-TAY (Devotee) – A person warmly devoted to something or someone..

DEXTEROUS – Skillful in the use of the hands. Having mental skill or adroitness.

DIMINUTIVE – Extremely small in size; tiny.

DISCERNING – To perceive with the eyes or intellect; detect. To recognize or comprehend mentally.

DISTINGUISHED – Characterized by excellence or distinction; eminent. Dignified in conduct or appearance.

DIVA – An operatic Prima Donna. A female singer.

DONNYBROOK – An uproar; a free-for-all.

DON QUIXOTE – The hero of a romance novel by Miguel de Cervantes.

DOOZY – (Slang) Something extraordinary or bizarre.

DOSE – (Spanish) The number 2.

DOUBLOONS – Ancient Spanish coins.

DUDESICKLE – (Slang) A man.

DUTCHESS – The wife or widow of a duke.

DYNAMIC – Of or relating to energy or to objects in motion. Marked by intensity or vigor; forceful, active.

DYNAMO – A generator. An extremely energetic or forceful person.

EDIFYING – Tending to instruct; to encourage intellectual, moral, or spiritual improvement.

ELAN – Enthusiastic vigor and liveliness with distinctive style and flair.

ELITE – The best or most skilled members of a group.

EL MAGNIFICO – The magnificent.

EL SUPREMO – The supreme.

EMPOWERMENT – To invest with power, especially legal power or official authority.

EMBARGO – A prohibition, a ban.

ENDEAVOR – A concerted effort toward an end; an earnest attempt.

ENLIGHTENMENT – The state of being enlightened. To be aware of and living in truth.

EPIC – An extended narrative poem celebrating the feats of a legendary hero. Surpassing the usual or ordinary, particularly in scope or size. Heroic and impressive in quality.

EPICENTER – The point of the earth's surface directly above the focus of an earthquake. A focal point.

Glossary

EPICURE – One who knows and heartily enjoys fine food and wine.

EPITHANY – A Christian feast celebrated on January 6. A comprehension or perception of reality by means of a sudden intuitive realization.

ERGO – (Latin) Therefore.

ESCALADE – The act of scaling a fortified wall or rampart; to climb.

ESTEEMED – To be appreciated and regarded with respect.

ERUDITE – One who is well instructed; learned.

EURYTHMIC – The art of interpreting musical compositions by rhythmical, free-style bodily movement.

EXCELLA-WOMAN-TAY – (Surfer slang) An excellent woman.

EXEMPLARY – Worthy of imitation; commendable.

EXEMPLIFY – To illustrate by example.

EXHILARATE – To invigorate and stimulate; to cause to feel happily refreshed and energetic.

EXISTENTIAL – Dealing with existence. Based on experience; empirical.

EXPEDITION – A journey undertaken by a group of people with a definite objective: "A chow expedition into the hinderland where the flavor rewards are vast."

EXPLOITS – Acts or deeds, especially brilliant or heroic ones.

EXQUISITE – Of such beauty or delicacy as to arouse delight; flawless – "an exquisite sunset."

EXTRAORDINAIRE – Extraordinary; beyond what is ordinary or usual.

EXUBERANT – Full of unrestrained enthusiasm or joy.

EXUDE – To emit gradually. To exhibit in abundance.

EXULTED – To rejoice greatly; be jubilant or triumphant.

FAH-BOO – (Slang) Fabulous.

FABULOSO – (Slang) Fabulous; extremely pleasing or successful.

FARFUGNUGGEN – (Slang) Fun; pleasure; enjoyment.

FLAMBOYANT – Richly colored; resplendent; showy; marked by striking audacity or verve.

FLAPDOODLE – (Slang) Foolish talk; nonsense.

FOMENT – To promote the growth of; incite.

Glossary

FOREFRONT – In the foremost part. The position of most importance, prominence, or responsibility; the vanguard.

FORSOOTH – (Early English) "In truth"

FRAULEIN – (German) - Used as a courtesy title in a German-speaking area before the name of a woman or girl. A woman.

FROLICKING – To behave playfully and uninhibitedly; romp.

FROULINE – (German) a single female.

FUSION – (Physics) A nuclear reaction in which nuclei combine to form more massive nuclei with a simultaneous release of energy.

GALVANIZING – To stimulate with electric current. To arouse to awareness or action; spur; "the issue galvanized the electorate."

GASTRONOMIC – Relating to the art or science of good eating.

GOETHE – German writer and philosopher. A master of poetry, drama, and the novel.

GOLD SOVEREIGN – A gold coin used in early England.

GOOD WILL AMBASSADOR – A non-official person who represents or spreads good will.

GOTHAM – New York City.

Wickhead's Guide to Verbal Gusto

GRAND DAM – Grand lady.

GRAND FROMAGE – Big cheese.

GREEN – A catchword denoting green living practices focusing on reducing pollution to the planet through: wind power, recycling, organic farming, etc..

GREEN ROOM (BOWLED, SHACKED, TUBED) – (Surfing) Terms which refer to riding across the wave face in the cylinder formed between the wave and the lip.

GRINDIN' (Slang) – Skateboarding across something with your board grinding against it, like some unbelievable handrail, for example.

GUMPTION – Boldness of enterprise, initiative, or aggressiveness; guts; spunk.

GURU – A personal spiritual teacher. A trusted counselor and advisor. A recognized leader in a field; "a guru of high finance."

GUSTO – Keen enjoyment; enthusiastic appreciation; zest.

GUSTO GRABBING – Vigorously reaching for enjoyment and pleasure.

GUSTO REPORT – Any research revealing where and when to find the utmost action and adventure.

HAMMISH – From the heart; true; authentic.

Glossary

HARBINGER – One that indicates or foreshadows what is to come; a forerunner.

HASTEN – To move or act swiftly.

HECTIC – (Surfing) Something radical, extreme.

HEED – To pay attention to; listen to, and consider.

HEEZY FO' SHEEZY – (Hip Hop) Slammin' cool. Off the hook energy, fun, style, etc.

HELIOPAUSE – The outer boundary of the universe.

HELM – The steering gear of a ship, especially the tiller or wheel. A position of leadership or control: "at the helm of the committee."

HERALDED – To be previously announced. To have one's approach or presence proclaimed.

HERCULES (Greek & Roman Mythology) – The son of Zeus and Alcmene, a hero of extraordinary strength who won immortality by performing 12 labors demanded by Hera.

HEROINE – A female hero.

HIGH FREQUENCIES – The vibrations caused by good thoughts which attract other high frequency things such as love, peace, joy, and success.

HIGH PANJANDRUM – An important or self-important person.

Wickhead's Guide to Verbal Gusto

HOMBRE – (Surfing) A man; a dude who goes for it!

HOUDINI – After Harry Houdini, the famous escape artist. To accomplish seemingly magical feats.

HUMANITARIAN – One who is devoted to the promotion of human welfare.

HUMDINGER – (Slang) One that is extraordinary or remarkable.

HYPOTHESIS – A tentative explanation that accounts for a set of facts and can be tested by further investigation; a theory.

ICON – An image; a representation. One who is the object of great attention and devotion; an idol.

IMBUE – Permeate; "The salsa imbues this burrito with flavor."

IMBUED – To inspire, permeate, or invade: "work imbued with the creative spirit."

IMPECCABLE – Having no flaws; perfect.

INCANDESCENT – Emitting light; shining brightly. Characterized by ardent emotion, intensity, or brilliance.

INCIPIENT – Beginning to exist or appear.

INCISIVE – Penetrating, clear, and sharp, as in operation or expression; "an incisive mind."

Glossary

INCITE – To provoke or urge on.

INDEFATIGABLE – Incapable or seemingly incapable of being fatigued; tireless.

INDISPENSIBLE – Not to be dispensed with; essential.

INDOMITABLE – Incapable of being overcome, subdued, or vanquished; unconquerable.

INGENUITY – Inventive skill or imagination; cleverness.

INIMITABLE – Defying imitation; matchless.

INDUBITABLY – Too apparent to be doubted; unquestionable.

INGENIOUS – Marked by inventive skill or imagination.

INGENUITY – Inventive skill or imagination; cleverness.

IN LIEU OF – Instead of.

INNATE – Possessed at birth; inborn. Possessed as an essential characteristic; inherent.

INSTANTANEOUS – Occurring or completed without perceptible delay; instantly.

INTELLIGENTSIA – In the intellectual elite of a society.

INTERFACE – A point at which independent systems or diverse groups interact. To interact or coordinate smoothly.

INTERFACING – A point at which independent systems or diverse groups interact.

INTERPRETER – One who translates orally from one language into another.

IT – Information technology.

IN VOGUE – To be in step with prevailing fashion, practice, or style. Popular acceptance or favor; popularity.

INTREPID – Resolutely courageous; fearless; brave.

JAM (Musical) - To play (or sing) with improvisation.

JAUNTY – Having a buoyant or self-confident air.

JAZZING THE GLASS – Ripping on glass surf.

JIGGAWATT – Mucho watts.

JIGGY – (Slang) Go for it; get into it; lose your inhibitions; vastly popularized by Will Smith's rap song, "Get Jiggy Wit It."

JOIE DE VIVRE – Hearty or carefree enjoyment of life.

JOVIAL – Marked by hearty conviviality and good cheer.

JAM OUT – Totally committed to achieving excellent results, whatever it takes.

Glossary

KINDRED SPIRIT – Having a similar or related origin, nature, or character. On the same wavelength as someone else.

KNIGHT ERRANT – A knight who wanders in search of adventures to prove his chivalry.

KOSHER – Genuine, authentic, legitimate.

KUDOS – A claim or praise for exceptional achievement.

LADEN – Weighed down with a load; heavy.

LIGHT YEAR – The distance light travels in a vacuum in one year, approximately 5.88 trillion miles. A long way.

LIEGE – A lord or sovereign in feudal times.

LILLIPUTIAN – Very small; diminutive; from Gulliver's Travel's by Jonathan Swift.

LITHE – Supple. Marked by effortless grace.

LOFTY – Of imposing height; elevated in character; exalted.

LOLLAPALOOZA – (Slang) Someone or something outstanding.

LUMEN – An international unit of light.

LUMINARY – An object that gives light. A person who's an inspiration to others. Someone who has achieved eminence in a specific field.

Wickhead's Guide to Verbal Gusto

MADEMOISELLE – (French) A single woman.

MAESTRO – A master in an art.

MAGIC WANDOO – A metaphor for the San Francisco Giants special breed of magic. Anything causing extraordinary magic.

MAGNANIMOUS – Courageously noble in mind and heart. Generous; unselfish.

MAGNATE – A powerful or influential person, especially in business or industry.

MAGNUM OPUS – A great work, especially a literary or artistic masterpiece.

MAHATMA – In India and Tibet, one of the class of persons venerated for great knowledge and love of humanity.

MAMBREENO (or MAMBRINO) – From Don Quixote, "the Golden Helmet of Mambreeno." Don believed once you put it on, you were invincible. Modern usage: anything one wishes to be magical and special.

MAMMOTH – Something of great size; enormous; huge.

MANDATE – A command or an authorization given by a political electorate to its representative.

MANIFEST – Clearly apparent to the sight or understanding; obvious.

Glossary

MAN OF LETTERS – A man who is devoted to literary or scholarly pursuits.

MANGO – The sweet, juicy ovoid fruit of the tropical mango tree. Also, a Chan Wemo metaphor for a "football."

MANY SPLENDORED – Brilliant and magnificent in many ways.

MARSHAL – To enlist and organize; "trying to marshal public support."

MATRIARCH – A mother or highly respected female head of a family.

MATRICULATE – To be admitted into a group, especially a college or university.

MAVEN – A person who has special knowledge or experience; an expert.

MAZALTOV – (Yiddish) Used to express congratulations or best wishes.

MELODIOUS – Agreeable to hear; tuneful; "a melodious voice."

MENSCH – (Yiddish) A person having admirable characteristics, such as fortitude and firmness of purpose.

MENTOR – A wise and trusted counselor or teacher.

MERIT – Superior quality or worth; excellence.

METAPHOR – A figure of speech where a word or phrase ordinarily designating one thing is used to designate another; thus, "All the world's a stage."

METROPOLIS – A major city, especially the chief city of a country or region.

MI AMIGO – (Spanish) My friend.

MILIEU – An environment or a setting.

MIRTH – Gladness and gaiety, especially when expressed by laughter.

MOGUL – A very rich or powerful person; a magnate.

MOJO – An indefinable quality of power, force, or momentum.

MON AMIE – (French) My love.

MON CHERIE – (French) My friend.

MOXIE – (Yiddish) The ability to face difficulty with spirit and courage.

MYRIAD MINDED – Possessing knowledge and interests in a vast array of subjects.

MYTHICAL – Of or existing in myth, "the mythical unicorn."

NAIVETÉ – The state or quality of being artless or uncritical. Lacking worldliness and sophistication. Gullible.

Glossary

NANOSECOND - One billionth of a second.

NE PLUS ULTRA - The highest point of excellence or achievement; the ultimate.

NIMBLE - Quick, light, or agile in movement or action; deft - "nimble fingers."

NOBLE MINDED - Showing qualities of high moral character such as courage, generosity, or honor.

NO NEGS - (Slang) No negative vibes.

NONPAREIL - Having no equals; peerless.

NOTEWORTHY - Deserving notice or attention; notable.

NUANCE - A subtle degree of difference, as in meaning, feeling, or tone: "a rich artistic performance full of nuance."

NUCLEAR FURNACE - The Sun.

OCHO - "The Ocho" Sports Channel 8 from the movie *Dodgeball.*

OMBUDSMAN - A person who investigates complaints and mediates fair settlements.

OMNIPOTENT - Having unlimited or universal power, authority, or force; all powerful.

OPTIMISTIC - A tendency to expect the best possible outcome.

Wickhead's Guide to Verbal Gusto

OPUS – A creative work, especially of musical or literary composition.

ORATOR – One who delivers an oration. An elegant and skilled public speaker.

PALADIN – A paragon of chivalry; a heroic champion. A strong supporter or defender of a cause.

PANACHE – Dash; verve.

PANJANDRUM – An important or self-important person.

PARADIGM – An example that serves as a pattern or model.

PARLAY – (Games) To maneuver (an asset) to great advantage.

PATRIARCH – A man who rules a family, clan, or tribe.

PATRON - One that supports, protects, or champions someone/something, such as an institution, an event, or a cause; a sponsor or benefactor: "A patron of the arts."

PAY IT FORWARD – An expression for describing the beneficiary of a good deed repaying it to others instead of the original benefactor.

PEGASUS - (Greek Mythology) A winged horse.

PEERLESS – Having no match; incomparable.

Glossary

PERSONA BOOM BROTTUS – (Slang) An esteemed and welcomed person.

PERSONA ROCK AND ROLLA – (Slang) One who rocks and rolls.

PERSPICACIOUS – Having or showing penetrating mental discernment; clear-sighted.

PHENOM – (Slang) A phenomenon, especially a remarkable or outstanding person.

PHILANTHROPIC – The effort to increase the well-being of humankind, as by charitable aid or donations.

PIASANO – (Italian) Country gentleman, comrade, or friend.

PIECE DE RESISTANCE – An outstanding accomplishment. The principal dish of a meal.

PINNACLE – The highest point; the culmination.

PIONEER – A person who goes before, preparing the way for others; as an early settler.

PITHY – Precisely meaningful, forceful, and brief.

PLAUDITS – Enthusiastic expression of praise or approval.

PLENIPOTENTIARY – Invested with or conferring full powers – "a plenipotentiary deputy."

Wickhead's Guide to Verbal Gusto

PLUCKY – Showing courage and spirit in trying circumstances.

PLUPERFECT – More than perfect; supremely accomplished; ideal.

PMA – Positive mental attitude.

POET LAUREATE – A poet acclaimed as the best in the land.

POETRY SLAM – A poetry recital, if not more so.

POISED – Balanced and composed.

POLE-VAULT - A field event in which the contestant jumps or vaults over a high crossbar with the aid of a long pole.

POO-BAH – One who holds high office.

POPPIN – (Slang) Good looking.

POPULIST – A supporter of the rights and power of the people.

POST HASTE – With great speed; rapidly.

POST-UP – (Slang) To hook up with.

POTENTATE – One who has the power or position to rule over others; a monarch. One who dominates or leads a group or an endeavor.

Glossary

PRACTITIONER – One who practices something, especially an occupation.

PRECEDENT – An act or instance that may be used as an example in dealing with subsequent similar instances.

PRECLUDE – To exclude or prevent (someone) from a given condition or activity.

PREEMINENT – Superior to or notable above all others; outstanding.

PREMIER – First in status or importance; principal; chief.

PRESCIENT – Knowledge of actions or events before they occur.

PRESTIDIGITATOR - One possessing manual skill and dexterity in the execution of tricks; sleight of hand.

PRESTIGIOUS – Having high standing among others; honor or widely recognized prominence; esteem.

PRETERNATURAL – Out of or being beyond the normal course of nature; differing from the natural. Surpassing the normal or usual; extraordinary.

PRIMA BALLERINA – The leading woman dancer in a ballet company.

PRIMO – Exceptionally good; premium.

PROACTIVE – Acting in advance to deal with an expected difficulty; anticipatory – "proactive steps to keep the jalopy running."

PRODIGIOUS – Impressively great in size, force, or extent. Extraordinary; marvelous – "prodigious profits."

PRODIGY – A person with exceptional talents or powers.

PROFESSOR EMERITUS – A professor who is retired but retains an honorary title corresponding to that held immediately before retirement.

PROFOUND – Coming from great depth; deep; far-reaching – "profound wisdom."

PROMONADE – A leisurely walk.

PROMULGATE – To make known by public declaration; announce officially.

PROPITIOUS – Presenting favorable circumstances; auspicious.

PROPONENT – An advocate.

PROSE – Ordinary speech or writing without metrical structure.

PROTÉGÉ – One who is under the protection or care of another, especially an influential person.

Glossary

PROVISO – A clause in a document making a qualification, condition, or restriction.

PRUDENT – Wise in handling practical matters

PSYCHED – To be in a positive and enthusiastic state of mind.

PUBESCENT – Reaching or having reached puberty.

PUNDIT – A source of opinion; a critic – "a baseball pundit." A learned person on a given topic.

PURVEYOR – One that furnishes provisions, especially food. One that promulgates something - "a purveyor of humorous anecdotes."

QUANTUM – A quantity or amount a specified portion.

QUANTUM LEAP – An abrupt change or step, especially in method, information, or knowledge.

QUINTESSENTIAL – The pure, highly concentrated essence of a thing. The purest or most typical instance; "the quintessential copywriter."

RACONTEUR – One who tells stories and anecdotes with skill and wit.

RAD – (slang) Radical.

RADIANT – Emitting bright light; glowing; beaming.

RAJA – A prince, chief, or ruler in India.

RAVISHING – To overwhelm with emotion; enrapture.

REGIMEN – A regulated system, as of: diet, therapy, or exercise; intended to achieve a beneficial effect.

REND – To tear or split apart violently. To pierce with sound.

RENDER – To submit or present. To perform an interpretation.

RENAISSANCE MAN – A man who has broad intellectual interests and is accomplished in areas of both the arts and the sciences.

RENDEZVOUS – A meeting at a prearranged time and place.

RENOWNED – The quality of being widely honored and acclaimed; fame.

REPARTEE – Conversation marked by the exchange of swift, witty retorts; lively talk.

REPLETE – Abundantly supplied; abounding.

REPOSITORY – A place of storage. A warehouse.

REPROACH – To express disapproval; criticism.

RESILIENT – The ability to recover readily.

Glossary

RESONATE – To exhibit or produce resonance or resonant effects. Spiritual - to be on the same frequency with personal truth and guidance.

RESPLENDENT – Splendid or dazzling in appearance; brilliant.

RETROGRADE – Moving backward; opposite to the visual order; reversed.

REVERED – To be regarded with awe, deference, and devotion.

REVERENT INGENUITY – Using clever action to not only achieve positive results, but also avoid any negative impact on a given system.

REVERSE SKEPTICISM – A tendency to find and focus on the good.

RHETORICAL – Of or relating to rhetoric, which is skill in using language effectively and persuasively.

RIDIC – (slang) Ridiculous.

RIFF – A short rhythmic phrase played on a musical instrument, especially one that is repeated in improvisation.

RIVETING – Wholly absorbing or engrossing one's attention; fascinating.

ROCK OF GIBRALTAR – A metaphor for an exceptionally strong person.

Wickhead's Guide to Verbal Gusto

SACRE BLEU (French) – An oath of being confounded. Oh gosh! Darn!

SAGACIOUS – Having or showing keen discernment, sound judgment, and far-sightedness; wise.

SALUTATION – A polite expression of greeting or goodwill.

SAMURAI – The Japanese feudal military aristocracy. Some one completely committed to a particular cause.

SANS – Without.

SALLY – To rush out or leap forth suddenly. To set out on a trip or excursion.

SALLY FORTH – To set out on a trip or excursion. To venture forth without reservation.

SAVANT – A learned person, a scholar.

SAVOIR-FAIRE – (French) The ability to do or say the right or graceful thing.

SAVVY – Well informed and perceptive; shrewd; "a savvy customer."

SCINTILLATING – To throw off sparks; flash; to be animated and brilliant.

SCRIBE – A public clerk or secretary, especially in ancient times. A writer or journalist.

Glossary

SCRUMP – (Slang) Scrumptious

SE MAGNIFIQUE – (French) Magnificent.

SEMANTIC – Of, or relating to, meaning; especially meaning in language.

SENORITA – (Spanish) An unmarried woman or girl.

SENSUOUS – Appealing to or gratifying the senses.

SHACKED – (Surfing) See green room.

SHERPA – Himalayan mountain people known for their skill and ability at mountaineering. Someone adept at skiing, snowboarding, mountain climbing, etc.

SHHH-WAIT, LOOSE BOW WOW – (Slang) "Drop everything, here comes an unleashed dog."

SHIBUMI – Authentic yet understated power, strength, or beauty.

SHIP'S CHANDLER – One who supplies a ship or situation with necessary supplies.

SHOW-STOPPER – A performance or performer that evokes so much applause from the audience that the show is interrupted.

SITCH – (Slang) Situation.

SKOOKUM – Really good; excellent.

Wickhead's Guide to Verbal Gusto

SMITHSONIAN – Our national museum in Washington D. C.

SMURF BARREL – (surfing) A miniature, perfectly formed barrel. Can also describe when a surfer takes off in a standing position, then flops down on the board to shoot through the tiny barrel.

SOCRATES – Greek philosopher who initiated a question-and-answer method of teaching as a means of achieving self knowledge.

SOULFUL – Full of or expressing deep feelings; profoundly emotional.

SPACE-TIME CONTINUUM – The four-dimensional continuum of one temporal and three spatial coordinates, in which any event or physical object is located.

SPLENDIFEROUS – Splendid.

SPONTANEOUS – Arising without apparent external cause; self-generated.

SPORTING GREEN – A place where outdoor sports are played. A literary publication dedicated to sports.

SPOUSE – A marriage partner; a husband or wife.

SPRUCE – Neat, trim, and smart in appearance.

SQUID LID – (surfing) The nickname for a neoprene hood used to counter the effects of cold air or water.

Glossary

STEADFAST – Fixed or unchanging; steady. Firmly loyal or constant; unswerving.

STELLAR – Of, relating to, or consisting of stars. Of or relating to a star performer. Outstanding.

STEWARD – One who takes care of another's property, finances, or other affairs.

STOKED – Exhilarated or excited; amped.

STORIED – Celebrated or famous in history or story – "the storied wisdom of Alfred E. Newman."

STRING THEORY – A cosmological theory based on the existence of cosmic strings.

SUAVE – Smoothly agreeable and courteous.

SUBLIME – Of high spiritual, moral, or intellectual worth. Not to be excelled; supreme.

SULTAN – A ruler of the former Ottoman Empire; a powerful person.

SUMMARILY – Performed speedily and without ceremony.

SUNDAY GO TO MEETIN' BUN – (slang) A leftover roll that one quickly pockets on the way to church.

SUPERB – Of unusually high quality; "a superb idea."

SUPERLATIVE – Of the highest order, superior to all others.

Wickhead's Guide to Verbal Gusto

SUPPLE – Moving and bending with agility; limber; flexible.

SURVEY – To examine or look at in a comprehensive way.

SVELTE – Slender or graceful in figure or outline; slim.

SWANK – Imposingly fashionable or elegant; grand.

SWASHBUCKLING – To act as a swashbuckler; a flamboyant swordsman or adventurer.

SYNC – Synchronization. Harmony; accord.

SYNTHESIZE – To combine as to form a new, complex product.

TABLEAU – A vivid or graphic description; a striking incidental scene.

TAPIOCA TWIZZLER – (surfing) A rowdy wave churned out by the belch of Neptune.

TECHNITION – An expert in a technique. One whose occupation requires training in a specific technical process.

TELEMETRY – The science and technology of automatic measurement and transmission of data by wire, radio, or other means from remote sources, as from space vehicles to receiving stations for recording and analysis.

TEMPORAL – Of, relating to, or limited by time: a temporal dimension; temporal and spatial boundaries.

Glossary

TENACIOUS – Holding persistently, holding firmly, strong.

TERRA INCOGNITA – (Latin) Unknown territory.

TITAN – A person of colossal size, strength, or achievement.

TOIL – To labor continuously; work strenuously.

TOP BANANA – (Slang) The person in charge; boss.

TOPFLIGHT – First-rate; excellent.

TOUR DE FORCE – A feat requiring great virtuosity or strength, often undertaken for its difficulty; "the report was a tour de force."

TOUTED – Promoted or praised energetically.

TRANSCENDENT – Surpassing others; preeminent.

TRES CHIC – (French) Fashionable; stylish. Adapting or setting current fashions and styles.

TRIBUNE – An officer of ancient Rome elected by the plebeians to protect their rights. A protector or champion of the people.

TRIBUTE – A gift or other acknowledgment of gratitude or admiration.

TRICKIN' – (Surfing) Performing tricky moves.

TROUBADOUR – A strolling musician.

Wickhead's Guide to Verbal Gusto

TUBED – (Surfing(See green room.

TUT, TUT – (Slang) Not to worry, it's easily dealt with.

UBER – (Slang) Trendy synonym for super – "uber delicious"

UNALLOYED – Pure; complete; unqualified; unadulterated.

UNEXCELLED – Not excelled by others.

UNPARALLELED – Without parallel, equal, or match; unequalled.

UNPRECEDENTED – Having no previous example; "an unprecedented volume of customers."

UNSURPASSED – Not passed by others.

URBANE – Refined and often elegant in manner.

URBANITE – A city dweller.

USHER – One who leads or guides. To precede and introduce.

VALEDICTORIAN – A student or person with the highest academic rank in a class.

VANGUARD – The foremost or leading position in a trend or movement.

VAUNTED – To be praised, to be spoken boastfully of.

Glossary

VENERABLE – Commanding respect by virtue of age, dignity, character, or position.

VERBAGE – Words.

VIBRANT – Pulsing or throbbing with energy or activity. Vigorous; lively and vital.

VICEROY – A man who is the governor of a country, province, or colony, ruling as the representative of a sovereign.

VICINITY – Being near or close by; nearness, proximity.

VIRTUOSO – A musician or person with masterly ability, technique, or style.

VISIONARY – A person who has vision and foresight. A seer of future possibilities.

VIVACIOUS – Full of animation and spirit; lively.

VOON-DER-BAR – (Slang) Terrific; good; wonderful.

WAHINI (Wa-hee-nee) – (Hawaiian) Woman.

WARRIOR-CHIEFTAIN – A chief of a tribe who is engaged or experienced in conflicts.

WAYFARING – Traveling; especially on foot.

WILEY – Full of wiles; cunning.

Wickhead's Guide to Verbal Gusto

WOOKIE – A tall, hairy humanoid in the *Star Wars* fictional universe.

WUNDERKIND – (German) A child prodigy. A young person of exceptional talent or ability.

YON – (Old English) Yonder; being at a distance indicated or known.

ZENITH – The point of culmination; the peak: The zenith of her career.

Author's Bio

Jim Kelly (JK) spends most of his time at Larson Family Winery in Sonoma, California. Prior to the winery, he worked as an advertising copywriter in Chicago. While in the windy city, he took an improv class at Second City ... he has yet to put it back. *Wickhead's Guide to Verbal Gusto* is his first book.

Dare I Say It?

For purchasing this resource, which can't help but raise the energy of the planet, there's no doubt in my mind that you are a tuned-in, free-thinking, gusto-grabbing, multifaceted *tour de force*.

May the *bon mot* be with you!

www.ingramcontent.com/pod-product-compliance
Lightning Source LLC
LaVergne TN
LVHW010300260326
834688LV00044B/1377